THE
UNWRITTEN LAWS
OF FINANCE
AND INVESTMENT

THE
UNWRITTEN LAWS
OF FINANCE
AND INVESTMENT

Robert Cole

P
PROFILE BOOKS

First published in Great Britain in 2010 by
PROFILE BOOKS LTD
3A, Exmouth House, Pine Street
London EC1R 0JH
www.profilebooks.com

First South Asian Edition 2010

ISBN 978-1-84668-254-4

Printed and bound by Gopsons Papers Ltd., Noida

CONTENTS

INTRODUCTION

In 2008 and 2009, as this book was being written, a financial crisis was consuming the world. A monetary disaster, the like of which had not been seen since the Great Depression of the 1930s, had struck. Banks, the institutions which create, distribute and collect most of the world's money, failed. Cornerstones of the financial system, such as mortgage lenders and insurance companies, crumpled and stock markets tumbled in the wake. Economic growth, the fire which warms standards of living across the globe, died away. Bankers, company executives, professional advisers and investors of all sorts were exposed as high-class fools, steeped in a pay-and-bonus culture that was flawed, thoughtless, arrogant and doomed. Capitalism faced testing questions.

Would greater familiarity with the facts of financial life have made a difference? Would people have got into as much trouble if they had taken more notice of the lessons of history? Would raised awareness of the dangers that lie in unbridled market forces have softened the manic market tendencies, replaced foolishness with wisdom, shown the value of sustainable investment and diluted the greed? Greater awareness of the eternal truths that lie at the heart of investment and finance would have helped people to avoid the worst. It would have helped people to understand and tackle the difficulties as they arose, finding routes away from crisis and the social unrest that can erupt alongside. Professionals should have known better and, for a time, the bruises will remind them they need to improve in future. If private individuals are to avoid loss in future crises – and it is almost certain that the darker part of financial history will repeat itself – they must surely learn the rules of the game.

Blessed with knowledge, people can better assess their options. Some will run a mile, concluding that the most sensible law of finance and investment was set out by William Shakespeare when, in *Hamlet*, he had Polonius say, 'Neither a borrower nor a lender be.' But, as this short book shows, it needn't be like that, and the dangers posed by burying one's head in the sand are greater than facing up to the risks that come with attempts to secure an adequate standard of living.

Casual observers may find investment and finance hard to fathom. The subjects can be confusing, frustrating and annoying. Puzzling contradictions and paradoxes are occupational hazards. Rules and laws that apply in some circumstances may not apply in others. Some apparently contradictory laws may need to be considered simultaneously. Depending on circumstances, some rules are more useful than others. As in life, rules are also made to be broken, occasionally, and sometimes exceptions prove their value. It is invariably necessary to balance opposing facts, guidance and analysis. Few investment decisions can be drawn in black and white; most involve judging the relative merits of a spectrum of colours and shades.

The Unwritten Laws of Finance and Investment is written as a primer for the uninitiated and a refresher course for those with experience. It is split into six sections, adopting a structure designed to move readers from the introductory basics to guidance for those who wish to operate at higher levels.

The first three sections — 'Grandmother's Wisdom', 'Laws for the Innocent' and 'Laws for the Cautious' — give guidance at its broadest and most approachable. As the book unfolds, through sections entitled 'Investment Laws', 'Laws of Finance' and 'Axioms of Experience', more detailed and sophisticated principles come into view. Some of the maxims covered in the early stages will be revisited, expanded, finessed and/or given wider contextual relevance.

'Grandmother's Wisdom' contains the easy-to-overlook simple truths. Familiarity need not breed contempt for the ageless classics, handed down from generation to generation. Section Two, 'Laws for the Innocent', contains principles that newcomers to the world of finance and investment must learn to understand (and that experienced investors should learn to remember). The third section is dedicated to risk, to the care that all investors must take to protect and enhance their financial security.

The 'Laws' included in the fourth section focus on markets and the nature of investment. It will help readers to develop better comprehension of the way markets work (and how they sometimes do not work), as well as giving insights into the way investments are valued. Section Five, 'Laws of Finance', explores the principles of finance. It is designed to improve practical proficiency and raise confidence by outlining the nature of what lies beneath the surface.

In 'Axioms of Experience', the last section, the focus swings back to the immediate concerns of investors and reverts to the proverbial tone set in the first section. With knowledge and application results improve. There is, this section emphasises, no substitute for experience.

There is a conceit at the heart of this book. Although it is called *The Unwritten Laws of Finance and Investment*, these laws are of course being written down here. And, in truth, many of them have appeared elsewhere, in some shape or form, so I owe a deep debt to all those who preceded me in endeavours to explain and codify the webs of laws, rules of thumb, tips and facts of financial life. But while many of the laws may be written elsewhere, most need explanation. My ambition is to put the eternal wisdom of finance and investment together in one helpful volume.

*

My thanks are due to many people and a wide range of sources. There is a debt to be paid to *The Global-Investor Book of Investment Rules*, with contributions from luminaries including Niall Ferguson, one of the most eminent financial historians of the age, Charles Schwab, who founded and gave his name to one of the world's best-known retail stockbrokers, and Robert Peston, who at the time of writing is the business editor of the BBC. It also includes contributions from people who are less well known and, as it happens, from me. Indeed, the opportunity I was given to pen my 'Tempus Golden Rules' in that volume led me, in a roundabout way, to embark on this larger project.

Some of the thoughts expressed here first appeared in columns I have written for *The Times* over the last decade and for the *London Evening Standard* and the *Independent* before that. Many came to me thanks to the work I undertook as a part-time lecturer in financial journalism at the City University in London, and in the process of writing a book (*Getting Started in Unit and Investment Trusts*, John Wiley, 1997) and a book-length web resource on buying shares, undertaken for an organisation called Equity Education.

I have been influenced by the *101 Golden Rules for Investors* written by a superbly well-informed and fair-minded consumer champion, David Cresswell. These rules, first published in 1995 under the auspices of the Investors Compensation Scheme, have not aged and they deserve a wider audience. I am grateful to Bernice Cohen, whose books *The Armchair Investor*, *The Money Maze* and *The Edge of Chaos* are stuffed with fantastic material. Ditto Michael Brett's *How to Read the Financial Pages*: it has a decent claim to be one of the best and most widely bought introductions to investment markets and money.

Other books I would like to acknowledge, and recommend as further reading, include Philip Coggan's *The Money Machine: How the City Works*; Jared Diamond's *Guns, Germs and Steel*; Jeffrey Frieden's *Global Capitalism*; Tim Hale's *Smarter Investing – Simpler Decisions for Better Results*; Sir Oscar Hobson's *How the City Works*; Angus Maddison's *Contours of the World Economy 1–2030 AD*; James Surowiecki's *The Wisdom of Crowds*; and Nassim Taleb's *Fooled by Randomness*.

I acknowledge the wisdom of investors such as Walter Bagehot, Anthony Bolton, Warren Buffett, Tom Dobell, Tony Dye, Philip Fisher, Milton Friedman, J. K. Galbraith, Benjamin Graham, Carl Icahn, Jesse Livermore, Peter Lynch, Adam Smith, George Soros and Nils Taube. The contribution to the field of artists and thinkers such as Sun Tzu, William Shakespeare, Leonardo da Vinci, Immanuel Kant and David Hume should also be acknowledged. Thanks are due from me to Murad Ahmed, Chris Ayres, Martin Barrow, Lorna Bourke, Ian Brunskill, Heather Connon, Sean Coughlan, Ian Cowie, Martin Dickson, Hugo Dixon, Clare Dobie, Jamie Doward, Ian Griffiths, James Harding, Anthony Hilton, Sarah Hogg, Chris Hughes, William Keegan, Barry Riley, Graham Searjant, David Smith, Hugh Stephenson, Tom Stevenson, Matthew Wall, Patience Wheatcroft, Terry Wilkinson and Martin Wolf.

I am also grateful to John Coggon, Emma Cole, Gwen Cole, Lucy Luck and especially Daniel Crewe, my editor at Profile Books, for advice, encouragement and support.

Grandmother's Wisdom

It is easy to ignore simple truths, or brush them aside. Financial history is littered with examples of men and women who failed to appreciate the power of obvious, common-sense principles. Familiarity breeds contempt for ageless classics, handed down by word of mouth from mother and father to son and daughter, but dog-eared usage suggests that these laws are reliable and informative.

Never forget rule number one

Warren Buffett, a stock market guru whose fame matches his status as an investor *par excellence*, says that the most important rule of investment – his first rule – is not to lose money. 'Rule number two,' says Buffett, is, 'Never forget rule number one.'

Most people assume that successful investment is about making money, but it is just as important to avoid loss. Since many if not all forms of investment are to some extent risky, it is almost inevitable that investors will incur losses from time to time. The fact that losses are such an occupational hazard means that investors must be constantly aware of the danger and work to avoid loss at all times.

Patience is a virtue

Actress Mae West said, 'Anything worth doing is worth doing slowly.' In investment, time is a great healer and a generous benefactor. Good investors – who are often sufficiently socially responsible to look askance at quick bucks made at other people's expense – think in terms of time horizons that stretch out for years. Contrary to what may be thought by those who see wheeler-dealer whizz-kids playing fast and loose with global capitalism, and who have the very short term in mind, a decade may be no more than a single unit of investment time. Good results are worth waiting for.

There is no such thing as a free lunch

If something looks too good to be true, the chances are it is too good to be true. Moreover, things that really are free often turn out to be worthless.

A penny saved is a penny earned

Bill Gross, the founder of PIMCO, the Pacific Investment Management Company, one of the world's largest investment companies, said, 'You must work intensely to keep your investment expenses as low as possible.'

You only need to look at the sums to see the financial damage done by fees. Say you have £1,000 and you earn 5 per cent a year of investment profits. Helped by the compounding of interest, the total earned over five years will be about £275. But what if start-up charges reduce the original £1,000 to £950 and management fees reduce the 5 per cent annual returns to 4 per cent? Both sets of fees look small but after five years the investment profit will be cut almost in half – from £275 to £155.

The key message here is not just that you should keep expenses low – that much is obvious – but also that you have to 'work intensely' on costs. Fees and charges come in all sort of guises and it is surprisingly easy to let them mount up. It is also surprisingly easy to ignore them, or be unaware of them.

It is necessary to remember all costs: the dealing fees for selling as well as buying; penalty fees that may kick in if you sell before the end of a pre-agreed investment term; the costs of advice; the costs of information; and the time of, say, an accountant whom you may need to help with book-keeping or tax returns.

All that glisters is not gold

'He who wishes to be rich in a day will be hanged in a year,' said Renaissance man Leonardo da Vinci.

Get-rich-quick schemes are as useless as they are commonplace. Theft and fraud give only illusory returns. Even on those rare occasions when a crime does pay, the few benefit at the expense of the many and that is a model that cannot last. Lotteries aren't much better: though legal, the odds on winning are stacked against the player. Big prizes are accompanied by the almost certain risk of disappointment, while small prizes are paid out to those prepared to suffer at least partial loss. At odds of about 14 million to one, there is more chance a British Lotto player will die in the half an hour before the draw takes place than scoop the main prize.

There are, however, investments that appear to resemble lotteries, such as British or Canadian Premium Bonds, that give variable returns depending on the luck of the draw. The difference is that lotteries take money away from investors overall, while Premium Bonds give money away net. Since there are plenty of small prizes, Premium Bonds can be a perfectly sensible, low-risk way of saving. If you have enough saved in Premium Bonds and wait with patience, returns can get close to 'normal' interest rates, although the existence of a big prize dilutes the size of other payouts.

Appearances can be deceptive

Just as it is rarely a good idea to judge a book on the strengths of its cover, so it is necessary to cut through the veneers of jargon and marketing-speak that often encase genuine investment opportunities. Simple logic lies at the heart of most, if not all, sound financial arrangements. Find the common-sense reasoning and investment success will follow.

You must speculate to accumulate

Little can be achieved unless you are prepared to run some degree of risk. As Emperor Napoleon Bonaparte observed, 'If you risk nothing, you gain nothing.'

The explorer Christopher Columbus crossed the Atlantic in 1492 in an attempt to find a westward route to the spices, silks and trading riches that came from India and China. The sea routes east were long, via the stormy Cape of Good Hope, while the Ottoman Empire blocked access through the Mediterranean and overland. Yet as a result of Columbus's accidental venturing, Europe laid claim to a whole New World. Columbus's trip ranks among the most successful investments ever made, but fear beset some of his would-be backers. The voyage was funded, only at the third time of asking, by Ferdinand and Isabella, Catholic monarchs of Aragon, Castile and Leon in Spain. It is thought King John II of Portugal was given the opportunity to invest as early as 1484, but declined. If only he had speculated he would have accumulated.

Don't put all your eggs in one basket

Don't just buy shares or stick your money in the bank. Don't stash it all in property or bonds, hedge funds, fine wine, ostrich farms or postage stamps. It is best to spread money about between so-called asset classes because it raises the chance of finding winners and reduces the risk of lumping on losers.

Imperial court jeweller Peter Carl Fabergé knew what to do with eggs. The gem-encrusted works of art that he created for the Russian royal family are so highly prized because each of them is decorated in its own fabulously extravagant way. One Fabergé egg is worth hundreds, if not thousands, of times its weight in pure gold. Indeed, all the world's Fabergé eggs together are worth approximately the same as all the tea in China. The damage caused by dropping a basket full of Fabergé eggs is hard to comprehend. If you put all your eggs – Fabergé or otherwise – in one basket you are running unacceptably large financial risks.

Well begun is half done

Beginning well is not just about selecting investments that take off. It is about securing foundations. Before you start investing, it is sensible to secure an income (that is, get a job) and to put a roof over your head. It is logical to pay off debt before starting to save. It is wise to kick things off with low-risk options. Start by putting aside some ready cash in a decent-paying bank deposit account. Then solidify the base by buying bonds and/or slices of commercial property. Then take on shares and finish off a portfolio by acquiring higher-risk so-called alternative assets, such as hedge funds.

It is important to get the basics right. Losing a pile

of money at the outset is more of a setback than giving up gains made later on. Good beginnings also breed confidence, which is as sound a commodity in investment as it is in other spheres. Meanwhile, those who start well are less likely to be alienated from a world that can be intimidating. 'A burned child dreads fire,' as Grandmother might say.

No news is good news

In finance and investment, as in life, damaging events are more arresting than happy ones. Bad news often comes suddenly and causes sharp falls in the value of investments, while good news accumulates and feeds incremental growth in the value of savings. It is important to look for the net impact. Consider, for instance, the Black Monday stock market crash of October 1987, which is held up as a typical illustration of the risks involved in equities. Despite falling by about a third in October and November of that year – an experience that is seared on the memory – many of the leading world stock market indexes ended that year higher than they started it.

Good investors keep a close eye on current affairs – financial and otherwise. Good investors learn the value of perspective and the necessity of remaining above the rough and tumble of rolling news.

Buyer beware

Or *caveat emptor*, as the Romans might have said. Not only are you your own best researcher, adviser and decision-maker, you are also your own best watchdog.

Do not expect investments to take care of themselves and do not expect others to act in your best interests. You may want to believe that governments offer protection and you may legitimise your expectations by pursuing claims through the press, through your elected political representatives or the courts.

Individuals are best placed to protect what is theirs and an individual's action is likely to be more effective than anything a government, a regulator or a compensation scheme might aspire to. You will lose if your investments lose value, so it is your lookout. Even if there is some sort of insurance or compensation available, it may give no more than partial restitution.

Don't panic

But if you do, panic early. If trouble strikes it is often best to act decisively and quickly to avoid loss, or to cut losses.

Numbers play tricks

'Not everything that can be counted counts,' said mathematician and physicist Albert Einstein, 'and not everything that counts can be counted.'

Consider the case of the share that drops in value by 50 per cent. It takes a rise of 100 per cent for it to get back to where it started. Consider also how it is possible for a share price to fall by 5 per cent a day for a year and still not become completely worthless. These are not difficult mathematical issues but they do show the importance of looking twice at figures to ensure that you do not thoughtlessly leap to the wrong conclusions.

When you are in a hole, stop digging

W. C. Fields, the American comedian, said, 'If at first you don't succeed, try, try again. Then quit. No use being a damn fool about it.'

It is important to accept errors and move on. It is one thing to learn from mistakes but quite another to dwell on them, to blow their significance out of proportion, or to allow them to derail your campaign to build long-term financial security.

Laws for the Innocent

While the wisdom learned from Grandmother is largely common sense, there are some less obvious principles that newcomers to the world of finance and investment should understand. Experienced investors forget them at their peril.

Ignorance is no excuse

Investors may complain about being left in the dark, but if money swills down the investment plughole the chances are it won't come back.

It is essential to read widely. Company reports are often bone dry, boring, long and over elaborate. But gems of information are to be found within the slurry of verbiage. It is important to read professional analysis and the small print of regulators' reports. The Internet gives investors easy access to information on a scale previous generations could only dream about, though some short cuts lie in respectable newspapers and financial news magazines.

Ask questions

David Cresswell, in his *101 Golden Rules for Investors*, gives a range of priceless advice. 'Don't be afraid to ask questions. It's your money and you want to know where it is going,' he writes. 'Quiz your financial adviser to check that he is working in your best interests.' Ask, 'Why is this investment right for me? Could I lose my money?' Expect your financial advisers to provide regular progress reports, in writing, and if you don't understand something, ask the firm for clarification. Then keep on asking, he says, until you are happy that you do understand it.

It is not only advisers whom investors must interrogate; it is company executives, fund managers, governments and analysts. You need to question what they say and what they write. You also need to question any numbers they may use, for, as the Victorian Tory statesman Benjamin Disraeli said, invoking author Mark Twain, 'There are lies, damned lies and statistics.'

The investor who asks a question may look like a fool for five minutes. The investor who does not ask questions endures a lifetime of foolishness. It is hard to overestimate the importance of being inquisitive and of asking impertinent and/or seemingly obvious questions.

Keep it simple

Albert Einstein said, 'If you can't explain it simply, you don't understand it well enough.' It is excellent discipline to test anyone, including yourself, against plain-as-day criteria. Could you explain to someone else why you decided to invest, or not to invest? Would your partner in conversation and/or an eleven-year-old child find the explanation convincing? Exotic ingredients may be exciting, but simple truths almost invariably lie at the heart of sound finance and good investment.

Simple things are not necessarily simplistic

It is tempting to mistake complexity for sophistication and sophistication for quality. In fact, most – if not all – sound investments are based on simple, powerful and logical truths. Complexity can confuse or hide the important essence. Meanwhile, there are few things more simplistic than to assume that something is clever because it looks clever.

It is relatively simple to appreciate that the capital value of investments is closely linked to the profits, or income, generated. It is harder to decide which number accurately reflects underlying and sustainable profitability. How is profit related to value? Should you buy an asset for the equivalent of ten years' earnings? Or twelve? Or twenty? Similarly, dividends are simple payments to shareholders, but the implication of a change in the corporate policy towards dividends is far from simplistic.

Martin Whitman, one-time chairman of Third Avenue Management, the money management firm, said, 'Based on my own personal experience – both as an investor in recent years and an expert witness in years past – rarely do more than three or four variables really count. Everything else is noise.'

Jargon is the camouflage of charlatans and con artists

Some people are led astray because they do not understand. Others enrich themselves by pulling the wool over others' eyes. It may be possible to ride a mustang of complexity for a time: talk of collateralised debt obligations, credit default swaps and algorithm-based investment strategies hoodwinked plenty in the run-up to the credit crunch of 2008. But when the too-clever-by-half investment edifice collapsed, it was not the common-sense investors who were exposed and impoverished.

Be prepared to pay for knowledge

An experienced and dedicated investment adviser is worth any reasonable fee levied. The same goes for the cost of a subscription to a decent database, an investment manual or book. Money spent on efficient administration reaps rewards too. There is always a danger of shelling out for shoddy information or advice and 'If you pay peanuts,' as the oft-used idiom has it, 'you get monkeys.' But an investment in information is a prerequisite for those seeking financial returns.

It is worth considering whether you can earn more doing what you do in your main line of work – be it bricklaying or chartered surveying – than it costs you to get someone else to manage your money; if you can the costs are worth swallowing. Adam Smith, the Age of Enlightenment economic philosopher, first noticed the productive power of specialisation in his 1776 work *The Wealth of Nations*. A specialist or expert can achieve much more, much more quickly and cheaply, than a novice or a generalist.

Analysis without evidence is guesswork

Peter Lynch, the professional investment manager who did much to establish the reputation of Fidelity, one of the world's largest investment management groups, said, 'Investing without research is like playing stud poker and never looking at the cards.'

Personal and professional investment circles are riddled with people who ignore factual evidence and who, because they allow prejudice to take over, are directed by guesswork and whim. People often believe what they want to believe, in rank disregard for reality. For centuries it was thought that the application of blood-sucking leeches played a central role in helping sick people to recover their health. *Hirudo medicinalis* was widely used, from ancient times right up until the early nineteenth century. Without evidence, medieval medics guessed that all manner of illnesses could be cured by sucking blood from ailing men and women. Modern medicine, thanks to the empirical science of William Harvey and others, discovered that lifeblood should be cherished. Investment – in the sense that it facilitates the transfer of money, and so ideas, around the world economy – is lifeblood. Without rigorous examination and evidence, clots are created.

Appreciate the difference between price and value

According to playwright Oscar Wilde, 'A cynic is someone who knows the price of everything and the value of nothing.'

It is rarely easy to attribute either price or value to financial assets with certainty, but whereas prices can fluctuate wildly, value shifts more slowly. Value, while not fixed in stone, is less vulnerable to feckless changes in market sentiment. Investors who take a firm grip on valuation will be able to tell the difference between a price that is expensive and one that represents a bargain.

Happily prices and values normally converge over the long term, but it is best to take the ups and downs of day-to-day pricing with a large pinch of salt. Warren Buffett's plain-as-day philosophy led him to see value in Coca-Cola shares because he liked the taste of Cherry Coke. He worked on the assumption, 'Price is what you pay. Value is what you get.'

Buy low, sell high

Harry Enfield, the British comic, invented a screen character called Tim Nice-But-Dim. An upper-class twit, Nice-But-Dim was seen in one sketch giving his bank manager some financial advice. 'Buy high, sell low,' he said, 'or have I got that the wrong way round? Course I have ... sell low, buy high.'

The skit illustrates just how easy it is to get the rule back to front, not only in comedy but in practice too. We forget at our peril that good investments are bought at low prices and sold at high ones; that bad investments are bought at the top and sold at the bottom. The secret to success is to master the difficult task of judging what precisely constitutes 'high' and 'low'.

There is a difference between investment and gambling

To some, an investment is a gamble. You might decide to put your shirt on the outcome of the Kentucky Derby in the hope of getting three shirts back the same afternoon. Or you might invest in a company that sells southern or Kentucky fried chicken, hoping to turn £100 into £300 over the course of ten years. Are these things the same? No. One is a gamble and the other an investment.

There is often more to investment than making simply financial returns, while it can also be self-defeating to focus exclusively on profit. Through investment, jobs are created, satisfaction comes to customers and tax is paid to fund defence and social security obligations. Thanks to investment, societies achieve all-round progress. With investment, all can win. Gambling, while it gives money to some, creates lots of losers as well. There is also a big difference between stock market gamblers – sometimes known as day traders – who buy and sell with the aim of gaining from short-term market movements, and investors, who provide capital with a view to benefiting from the longer-term underlying economic expansion of companies and countries.

Create your own luck

Niccolò Machiavelli, the Italian philosopher and politician, reportedly felt that success mostly came about because of luck. The rest, he said, was bravura and cunning. The good investor works hard to create his or her own luck by researching, observing, learning and acting intelligently, carefully and firmly.

Investors create their own luck by avoiding trouble, just as pedestrians avoid the bad luck of being hit by a falling paint tin by walking around, rather than underneath, ladders. Equally, investors might avoid the 'bad luck' of being hit by adverse movements in the foreign-exchange market by keeping only modest sums in overseas investments, or by balancing the risks of one currency with another.

It is easy to believe that investment success comes about through skill and sound judgement, while failure boils down to bad luck. Pure luck might just as easily bring success, while failure frequently comes as a result of poor skills and flawed judgement.

Markets are driven by fear and greed

One of the mantras of Berkshire Hathaway, the investment fund of Warren Buffett and Charlie Munger, is, 'We simply attempt to be fearful when others are greedy and to be greedy only when others are fearful.'

The allure of making easy money is as powerful as the fear of losing it, yet this quote neatly illustrates two laws: first, that fear and greed are among the most powerful of investment forces; and second, that it is often a good idea to act against the grain of popular opinion.

Ride the tides

A rising tide lifts all boats, according to one of the oldest of stock market axioms. Investment is never easy, but it is easier to succeed when the economic environment is benign. When the general stock market mood is sound and confidence is flowing freely, profits come. But when the stock market tides ebb, good investments suffer alongside bad ones; and it is when the tide goes out that the wrecked hulks of erstwhile dreams are revealed. As Warren Buffett said, 'It's only when the tide goes out that you learn who's been swimming naked.'

Practically, this means that investors should learn to enjoy, and profit from, the good times but not become overconfident in their own abilities to achieve success in the good times. Nor should they despair in the bad times, or lose confidence, although it is only sensible to act more cautiously when the investment waters are flowing against you. In addition, investors should be wary of those who profess to have special powers or special talents. Though individual skills are important, upbeat market conditions can make the most foolish investor look wise.

Expect the unexpected

Surprises and investment go hand in hand, and while there is little one can do to avoid unexpected events, good investors know that they must be prepared to deal with unforeseen and unforeseeable events.

Unexpected things will happen, as the work of Nassim Taleb, the writer who made a fortune first from trading stocks and then by writing *Fooled by Randomness* and *The Black Swan*, suggests.

Reality is drenched in uncertainty. With investment, as with life, rare types of luck, or misfortune, may only occur infrequently, but there are lots of different rare events that could strike, with significant consequences. As Taleb says, long periods of calm breed complacency; the sense of expectation is dulled by the absence of the unexpected. It is through diversification and keeping portfolios under constant review that investors can best prepare for unexpected events.

Section Three

Laws for the Cautious

At the heart of all sound investment practice is the management of risk. Prudent people, however, know it is necessary to embrace uncertainty, not to eliminate it, because the elimination of danger reduces, or even destroys, the opportunity to make money. The following laws give guidance on treading the fine line between risk and reward.

Embracing uncertainty

It is only natural to want steadiness, simplicity and security. As with life, however, investment is inherently unpredictable. That said, some hazards can be avoided, while others cannot be dodged and must be accounted for. Some perils can be foreseen, but others are invisible. It is all too easy to assume that something will happen and then it doesn't, just as it is easy to assume something will not happen and then it does. There is a difference between jeopardy and opportunity, chance and good fortune.

Investors naturally dislike uncertainty because it is threatening, dangerous and risky. At the same time it was Robert Fitzhenry, the Canadian publisher, who said, 'Uncertainty and mystery are energies of life. Don't let them scare you unduly, for they keep boredom at bay and spark creativity.'

It is often better to travel than to arrive

Uncertainty is a key investment commodity, because investment opportunities usually evaporate by the time events prove predicted answers right or wrong. Investment markets invariably look to the future: investors make money by correctly anticipating how future events will affect the value of their savings.

Diversification is a golden rule

Wise investors know that their judgements are fallible and insure themselves against unforeseen circumstances by keeping their fingers in lots of different pies. Save money in bank deposits, bonds, property, shares and, perhaps, more exotic things. Own a spread of investments within each asset class and ensure that you capture the benefits of geographical diversity.

Look for class

There are five broad classes of investment asset: cash, bonds, property, shares and so-called 'alternative' assets. They are listed here in ascending order of risk.

Cash is easy to see and easy to use – it is, to employ the jargon, liquid. Investors hold cash to pay for the everyday costs of living and as an emergency fund to meet the cost of unexpected events. They keep a reserve of cash to draw on to take advantage of investment opportunities when they arise.

It is important to recognise that deposits are not risk-free – a fact appreciated, in particular, by those who invested with the Icelandic banks before the crash of 2008. As with most investment-related truths, higher rewards suggest higher risk. Inflation, meanwhile, can erode the real value, or purchasing power, of cash.

Interest paid on cash deposits normally rises and falls in proportion to the rate set by a central bank

– that is, the Federal Reserve (or Fed) in the United States, the Bank of England in the UK and the European Central Bank (ECB). Commercial banks and savings institutions may pay less, or occasionally more, than the official rates, with the differences boiling down, largely, to judgements about credit risks and the competition for business between banks.

Bonds are best thought of as IOUs that, after issue, can be bought and sold second-hand – and also third-, fourth- and fifth-hand.

Buyers of bonds effectively lend money to governments and companies which, in turn, make promises to repay the sums with interest. In the second-hand market, bonds trade at prices set by the different investors who are buying and selling. Usually, bonds have a pre-agreed life span and pay interest, known as a 'coupon', at a level fixed at the outset. Because the market price of the bond can change, however, the effective rate of interest also shifts. Say an investor buys £100 of bonds which pay £5 a year in interest. Because bonds are bought and sold subsequent to issue in the open market, the price does not necessarily stay at £100.

If £5 a year is thought generous (as it might be if general interest rates go down), investors might pay more than £100. Conversely, if general interest rates rise, or the issuing company or government looks as if it might become unable to meet its repayment obligations, the price of bonds is likely to fall. As the price changes, the relative value of the £5 coupon also moves: expressed as interest or 'yield', £5 becomes 5.5 per cent if the market value of the bond falls to £90, just as the yield falls to slightly over 4.5 per cent if the market value of the bond rises to £110.

If you hold a bond for its entire life the effective yield will not change, because you will be repaid by the issuer in accordance with terms set at the outset, not in relation to the changing market value.

Bonds are suited to those who want steady streams of income and find the risks of shares too much to bear. Governments usually have sound credit records, especially ones such as those based in Washington, Tokyo, Canberra, Frankfurt and London. Companies, meanwhile, are obliged to meet their obligations to bondholders before shareholders. The drawback with bonds is that they can lose value, in real terms, if inflation runs high. Moreover, the opportunity for profits is capped because in the final analysis a bond is a loan.

Bonds are often called 'fixed-interest securities', because the interest on the bonds (or security) is fixed at the outset. Although fixed-interest bonds are the most common type, floating-rate bonds and index-linked bonds also exist. Index-linked bonds pay interest at rates linked to the retail prices index (RPI) and are thus inflation-proofed.

Property is the third type of asset. With an obvious everyday use, its physicality is an advantage not lost on those who own their home.

Commercial property splits into four subdivisions: office, retail, warehouse and industrial. It is attractive because over time rental income can be expected to rise in line with, or ahead of, inflation. That said, maintenance costs dilute the attraction of property assets; so does the fact that it often requires substantial initial capital outlay and purchase may have to be funded by borrowing. It can be difficult to sell – unlike cash, property is an illiquid asset.

Shares, also known as equities, constitute the

fourth class of asset. As with bonds, investors put up money for companies by buying shares. Unlike bondholders, shareholders are part-owners of the underlying enterprise and the value of the shares, and the accompanying dividends (the equivalent of interest on bank deposits or the coupons on bonds), have an open-ended capacity to increase in value. On the downside, shareholders are the first to shoulder financial burdens in tough times. Dividends are cut before the coupons payable to bondholders. Share prices tend to fall further and faster than bond prices.

Alternative assets, the fifth asset class, are a catch-all. Generally assumed to be of the highest risk, they can be defined as assets which are admired for their capacity to provide short-term growth in capital value. Income generation is rarely a frontline consideration. Alternative investment assets include private equity and hedge funds. Private equity investors often buy companies that have fallen on hard times and attempt to increase value by restructuring their affairs. Hedge funds use complex financial instruments such as so-called derivatives and deploy complex dealing tactics such as short-selling which allows them to gain from falling asset prices. Both private equity and hedge funds often use large amounts of debt – sometimes known as gearing or leverage – to magnify investment returns, although the corollary is to raise the risks too. Other exotic or alternative investments include vintage wines, classic cars and fine art.

Yield comparisons teach volumes

Invaluable comparisons between asset classes are made by working out the income yields on different types of investment. If you divide the income (that is, the coupons from bonds, the rent from property or the dividends from shares) by the capital value, you get what is effectively an interest rate, although it is more commonly referred to as 'yield'.

High yields suggest low prices and low yields suggest high prices, although exceptionally high yields – calculated with reference to past payments

– should be taken as a danger sign. It may indicate that the market has reduced the price of an asset in the belief that future income will fall. High yields may also point to real or potential fraud, or arrant foolishness.

Balance your bets

Nils Bohr, the Danish physicist, said, 'Prediction is very difficult, especially if it's about the future.'

Because prediction is so difficult investors should set themselves up for all eventualities. This means, for example, finding shares that are likely to do well in lean economic times (shares in supermarkets and utilities, for instance), as well as those that will do well in better conditions (leisure companies or banks, perhaps). It means putting some money in safe-haven bonds, while also investing in higher-risk but potentially more rewarding equities. It means engag-ing in short-selling (the investment technique designed to draw advantage from falling prices), as well as in conventional investment techniques. It means buying gold, in case paper currencies devalue, but not going overboard, because paper assets have plenty of advantages too. It means owning US Treasury bills on the assumption that America retains its economic supremacy, while gaining exposure to China because of the thought that Uncle Sam will be eclipsed by the new entrepreneurs of the Middle Kingdom.

Watch your weight

Good investors ensure that a portfolio is appropriately weighted, asking not only whether an investment is good but also whether it is good for a particular portfolio.

As part of maintaining a well-diversified portfolio of investments you might start by deciding to hold equal amounts of money in cash, bonds, property, equities and alternative assets. Depending on your circumstances and preferences, you may then decide to 'weight' the portfolio away from, say, alternative investments and equities if your instinct is to be cautious, or away from cash and bonds if your aim is to protect savings from inflation and you want to chase genuine growth in investment values. Within each asset class, moreover, ownership decisions may be weighted in favour of, or in fear of, certain specific sub-varieties.

On the risk-reward scale, there is a world of difference between shares of a stock market tiddler and a large multinational company. In property, there is a big difference between a shopping centre, a domestic residence and a stretch of farmland. Government bonds are different from those issued by local municipalities. Corporate bonds are different again, and bonds issued by blue-chip companies are in a different league to those issued by small companies.

The rule of three

Think hard about the reasons for taking action. The rule of three also provides a double safety net. If the passage of time invalidates one of three good reasons for doing anything, or you change your mind about one, there are still two left.

Consider these three examples. For most people a house is the biggest investment they will ever make. It is tempting to justify a house purchase purely in terms of the investment potential. This is important, and may be the main reason for buying, but house purchase makes sense because – eventually – ownership brings the privilege of living in a place rent-free. Yet why not also acknowledge that you'd like to buy a house for the same reason you'd like to have a diamond ring or a new car? Because you want it.

Example two: if you are thinking about buying a share in a company, examine the price in relation to at least three fundamental benchmarks: (a) the earnings of the company, (b) the dividend payments and

(c) the net asset value. If the price makes sense relative to all three benchmarks, and there is no serious counteracting force, allow investment logic to rule.

Example three: sell an investment if or when (a) it has made money, (b) you can think of a better place to invest and (c) there is a real threat the price will fall.

Making assumptions is essential, and dangerous

You may assume, for example, that economies will grow over the long term and that a soundly based, well-diversified investment portfolio will grow with the economy as a whole. You may assume that government bonds bring risk-free returns and are a benchmark from which other investment prospects should be assessed. You may assume that inflation is a constant threat to the real value of money and canny investment can neutralise the risk. You may assume that legislative edicts – on anything from obligatory motor insurance to expanding Internet access – will provide certain companies with assured business opportunities. You may want to make assumptions about the standard of living you'd like to have, whether you want to pay for your children's education, even your life expectancy.

You may make assumptions about all these things and plenty of others besides. Crucially, however, good investors recognise that assumptions are glorified guesses which must be frequently and diligently reassessed.

It is necessary to make assumptions because investment and finance are surrounded by uncertainty. Investors who fail to make assumptions become stuck, like rabbits staring into the headlights of approaching cars, unable to take decisions because vision is obscured by swirling mists of information.

Choose quality over quantity

Although portfolio diversification is essential, it is also important to be discriminating.

A model portfolio may have no more than twenty or thirty individual investments in it, although some of those selections may be collective or pooled investments such as unit trusts or pension plans, which themselves invest across a range. Focus helps the development of specialist knowledge, while a narrowed focus also aids administration. As fund manager Philip Fisher once said, 'I don't want a lot of good investments; I want a few outstanding ones.'

Time brings its own risks

Just as it is important to reduce risk by holding a spread of different types of investment, it is important to reduce the risks posed by time. Yes, the best returns are made by investors who buy and sell at the most auspicious moments. But it is impossible for investors to get their timing precisely right always. Anyone professing the ability to get the timing of investment entries and exits perfectly and consistently right is either a liar or extraordinarily lucky.

In 1923, Edwin Lefèvre published a book called *Reminiscences of a Stock Operator*. Drawing on the investment philosophy of Jesse Livermore, one of the most influential stock market traders of the early twentieth century, Lefèvre writes, 'One of the most helpful things that anybody can learn is to give up trying to catch the last eighth – or the first. These two are the most expensive eighths in the world. They have cost stock traders, in the aggregate, enough millions of dollars to build a concrete highway across the continent.'

Drip feed money into and out of markets

Mark Twain, in his novel *Pudd'nhead Wilson*, wrote, 'October. This is one of the peculiarly dangerous months to speculate in stocks in. The others are July, January, September, April, November, May, March, June, December, August, and February.'

It is much easier, and better, to reduce the chance of buying or selling at a bad price (and increase the chance of buying or selling at a good price) by phasing entries and exits. As a general guide, you may revert to the rule of three: buy or sell in three stages to increase the likelihood of securing a fair price. Alternatively, monthly savings plans such as those arranged with pension plans provide a practical way of drip-feeding money into investments.

There is safety in small numbers

Risk can be reduced by ensuring that no single investment makes up any more than a small part – say, 10 per cent – of the total. Those that adhere to this rule reduce the damage done if fortune moves against an individual investment decision.

Big is not necessarily beautiful

From Enron to the Mississippi schemes of John Law and eighteenth-century France, from Bernard Madoff's $50 billion fraud back to the bubble of nonsense that grew around Britain's South Sea Company in 1720, the size of a company or venture gives no firm assurance of security. Indeed, the bigger they are, the harder they can fall.

Set modest goals

Peter Lynch of Fidelity enjoyed a reputation as a world-beating investment guru. He said, 'In this business, if you're good, you're right six times out of ten. You're never going to be right nine times out of ten.'

Meanwhile, compliance officers and regulators work on the basis that anyone who appears to arrive at 'right' answers more than 60 per cent of the time deserves close investigation. Such success, honestly wrought, is so unusual, and so difficult to achieve, that it raises suspicion that it was won by nefarious means.

Bernard Madoff, revealed in late 2008 as one of the most breathtaking fraudsters of all time, attracted misplaced respect because his investment record seemed to show steady and handsome outperform-ance. Wise heads smelt a rat, even if they could not quite identify where the rat lay. Many more buried their heads in the sand, preferring not to ask the awkward questions about how someone could tame investment uncertainties so successfully and so consistently. In truth, of course, he didn't and disaster – eventually – struck.

Do not expect to get everything right all the time. Set your sights on getting more winners than losers, making a modest profit in absolute terms, beating inflation and/or doing as well as, or just a bit better than, a stock market index. If you meet modest aims in most parts of a portfolio in most years, you will be feted as a world-beating investment guru.

Align your interests

As merchant navies became established over the course of the seventeenth century, ship owners learned to ensure that ships' masters, or captains, had a vested interest in bringing home the cargoes. Blood ties bound early masters of ships who were relatives of owners. Then masters were expected to make a financial investment in ships. Then sea captains were trained to uphold standards and be reliable. In all these ways the threat of piracy was marginalised, cargoes were bought and sold at keen prices, and ships' captains found the quickest, safest routes between ports.

Similarly, if you take investment advice, or farm out investment management to a professional person or firm, satisfy yourself that they are motivated to act in your best interests. It makes sense to pay a one-off fee if you require one-off independent financial advice. In different circumstances, it also makes sense to pay someone who actively manages your money by percentage-based commission, because it gives him or her an incentive to make your money grow in value. That said, it makes less sense to agree to large, increasing and open-ended financial awards, because huge commissions may lead managers to run unreasonable risks in the hope of hitting the jackpot.

Regulatory alignment counts too

Sanctions on failure are as important as rewards for achievement. Investments in 'Wild West' ventures may have the potential to make big returns, but there is greater risk investing in companies operating in countries where the rule of law is weak.

Seals of approval from recognised regulatory authorities suggest that finance professionals and their investment plans satisfy a minimum set of competency standards. Approval suggests that people or firms involved in investment and finance will not bite off more than they can chew. It indicates that they have adequate financial backing. A lack of regulatory approval, meanwhile, serves as a clear alarm signal.

It is worth remembering, of course, that regulators are far from perfect. In fact, they are often exposed as being deeply imperfect – notably in the lead-up to the 2008 credit crunch, on both sides of the Atlantic and in Asia. As with many other aspects of investment, regulatory authority gives neither a guarantee of success nor a guarantee of redress in times of failure. This is an especially important factor to consider when investing overseas or in unusual varieties of investment. Fewer investors would have been caught out by a 1990s fad for ostrich farms if more probing questions had been asked about regulatory credentials.

Guarantees are rarely guaranteed

The lure of the guarantee means that the label is habitually used by investment marketers. But ultimately there is nothing – beside death and taxes, of course – that comes with an absolute guarantee.

Where guarantees are offered they are only ever as sound as the guarantor. It is often thought that governments offer the safest forms of investment because they can back their promises with legislation, military might and tax revenues. Government-backed bonds are sometimes even referred to as 'risk-free' investments. But you only need to recall the history of revolutionary Russia around 1917 to appreciate that countries as well as companies default on their obligations from time to time.

Insurance is often dressed up as a guarantee but is, in fact, no more than a safety net which shifts risk from one person to another. It carries a cost that is borne somewhere along the line, usually by consumers. Moreover, insurers are far from infallible. AIG, the world's largest insurance company, became one of the largest victims of the 2008 credit crunch when it had to admit its inability to stand by its offers of guarantees.

Instead of seeking the security of absolute guarantees, it is often advisable for investors to accept risk and balance the different forms of investment to produce net benefits. Some investment companies offer special products that promise to pay a guaranteed return linked to the performance of an index, such as the Dow Jones Industrial Average, the FTSE 100, the Nikkei, Hang Seng or Dax. But the price of the guarantee is paid for somehow – in the loss of dividend income, perhaps.

In these ways, guarantees can sometimes impede as well as assure. The actor Clint Eastwood put the point quite succinctly: 'If you want a guarantee, buy a toaster.'

Reckless conservatives lose too

Long-run historical data – such as that outlined in the 'Equity Gilt Study', published annually by Barclays Capital, the investment bank – suggest that you can lose money by being overcautious. History indicates that cash held on deposit at banks or in bonds increases in value more slowly than long-run rates of inflation. Over time, cautious investors can get poorer because their savings lose purchasing power. In the long run, history suggests, equities and property fare better.

Before you go in, look for the way out

Among the Winnie-the-Pooh stories of A. A. Milne is an episode where the eponymous bear gets stuck in a rabbit hole. Pooh, Milne writes:

> started to climb out of the hole. He pulled with his front paws, and pushed with his back paws, and in a little while his nose was in the open again ... and then his ears ... and then his front paws ... and then his shoulders ... and then –
>
> 'Oh, help!' said Pooh. 'I'd better go back.'
>
> 'Oh bother!' said Pooh. 'I shall have to go on.'
>
> 'I can't do either!' said Pooh. 'Oh, help *and* bother!'

As Pooh found out to his cost, it is easier to get into a tight spot than to get out of one. New investments can be beguiling, while the process of selling, even if you avoid panicky retreat, is weighed down by the fear of missed opportunity. The conundrum is

made no less awkward because investment companies spend freely on marketing exercises designed to
separate you from your money but spend only a
small fraction of the amount smoothing your exit
route.

Pooh might not have got into trouble if Christopher Robin had prevented him from eating so much
honey and condensed milk. Arguably, Rabbit should
have known better than to offer the weak-willed bear
such fattening foodstuffs. Ultimately, however, Pooh
suffered discomfort and humiliation because he
lacked foresight. In similar fashion, it is easier to get
mixed up with investment schemes than extricate
yourself from them.

Put yourself in the other guy's shoes

If you are thinking of buying, ask yourself whether
you'd sell if the tables were turned. If you are
tempted to sell, pretend for a moment that you are on

the other side of the deal. If someone is asking for investment, examine the real reasons they want the money. If someone wants to buy something from you ask why they would want to.

Time and effort spent looking at a decision from an alternative standpoint are rarely wasted. Assessing likely motives and incentives by putting yourself in the other guy's shoes might change your decision, or confirm it.

Sleep at night

If you are the sort who is likely to worry seek out safe routes to financial security. Brian Dennehy, a respected investment adviser, succinctly summed up the position in a 2003 interview for a newspaper: 'You need to make a hard-nosed choice about whether you can cope with risky investments. If you can't sleep because of the worry, then sell.'

INVESTMENT LAWS

There are a handful of rules which pertain more specifically to the realm of investment. They apply in a variety of circumstances and are as useful to the private individual intent on saving for a rainy day as to the hard-working entrepreneur dedicated to building a business empire.

Invest in people

Good investors appreciate the *human* nature of finance and investment. People create wealth; they also process it and consume it, and the unbreakable links between money and people mean that you make money by investing in people.

The Irish statesman and philosopher Edmund Burke, in his *Speech on Economic Reform* (1780), said, 'The people are the masters.' Abraham Lincoln, in his inaugural address as US president in March 1861, said, 'This country, with its institutions, belongs to the people who inhabit it.' He might have gone further and said that his country and its wealth depend on the people who are its population.

It is almost invariably because of human error, meanwhile, that investments turn sour. Companies are not things; they are collections of people. Investment managers, in spite of all the computer models they employ, are not automatons; they are people. Identify good people and you will identify good investments.

Invest in integrity

In his 1958 book *Common Stocks and Uncommon Profits* the money manager Philip Fisher outlines fifteen criteria by which he judged companies whose shares he might buy. He tells investors to look hard at the products a company makes, its commitment to research and development, effective sales methods, profit margins and labour relations. His golden rule, however, stated, 'If there is a serious question of the lack of a strong management sense of trusteeship for shareholders, the investor should never seriously consider participating in such an enterprise.'

Hail the herd

The market has strength because, among other things, it is an effective forum for the amalgamation of information and intelligence. While many assume that the market is a thing – some sort of inanimate shadowy institution – it is, in fact, a large and diverse group of people. The combined intelligence, knowledge and analytical power of the many is far greater than even the most talented and insightful guru.

James Surowiecki, in his 2004 book *The Wisdom of Crowds*, makes a powerful case in favour of the perspicacity of market forces. He notes how, if you play guess-the-number with jelly beans in a jar, the average answer provided by a class of thirty students is often accurate to within a surprisingly small margin for error. Surowiecki applied the hypothesis to the popular *Who Wants to be a Millionaire?* television programme. Contestants who seek help from the studio audience, he writes, produced a correct answer 91 per cent of the time. The accuracy of advice from single 'phone-a-friend' experts was only 65 per cent.

The combined brainpower of hundreds or thousands of people is likely to be better than the intelligence of even the most gifted single individual. Surowiecki notes that groups of people, such as markets, are at their best when the individual members are independent, decentralised and diverse.

Markets make mistakes

Surowiecki reckons that people are comforted by conformity – and that it may be a neuroscientific fact of life that humanity seeks the security of consensus. Yet the conclusions drawn are not infallible, as testified by the succession of financial manias, from the South Sea Bubble to the rush to invest in sub-prime US mortgages. Group-think sometimes leads to disaster: Surowiecki notes that ants, which usually cooperate to make effective and efficient colonies, occasionally get stuck in a life-threatening 'circular mill'. If, by chance or cruel design, the ants start marching in a huge, single-file circle (circular mills of this sort can be several hundred metres in diameter), they will blindly walk themselves to death.

'One of the quickest ways to make people's judgements systematically biased,' writes Surowiecki, 'is to make them dependent on each other for information.' During the dot-com mania at the end of the 1990s investors fed off the artless, one-track assumption that the Internet would automatically lead to investment nirvana. While it is important to note that the web has changed the world, and created many fortunes, the path to wealth was not a simple game of follow-my-leader. When group-think makes the ants mindlessly play follow-my-leader, it is time to step aside. Carl Icahn, a feared corporate raider and admired stock market investor, said, 'When most investors, including the pros, all agree on something, they're usually wrong.'

Sentiment rules, OK?

Sentiment – or mood – constitutes one of the single biggest forces driving investment. Markets are susceptible to the vagaries of perception and human error. Try as one might to believe that investors act rationally and deliver good answers, experience indicates that people are often driven by things other than cold logic and sober good sense.

Successful investors acknowledge, and learn to understand, the importance of behavioural psychology for the movement of markets. They also adjust their behaviour for the risks presented and position themselves to take best advantage. George Soros, the man who famously bet millions against the Bank of England in 1992 and won billions, subtitled his best-selling book *The Alchemy of Finance* 'Reading the Mind of the Market'. In it he wrote, 'Not only do market participants operate with bias, but their bias can also influence the course of events.' In practice, this might mean suspending judgement on certain investments while you allow irrational market conditions to run their course.

Look for patterns

John Kenneth Galbraith, the chronicler of the 1929 Wall Street crash widely regarded as the finest economic historian of the twentieth century, saw financial disasters as sagas that followed predictable patterns. In the first instance stupid, or unlucky, investment decisions are laid bare. Next, the rogue traders, who may have started in good faith, are found out. Lastly, the sins of brazen embezzlers are discovered. Meanwhile, Sir John Templeton, one of the most successful UK investors of the late twentieth century, a man who secured fame for his accurate analysis of the 1987 stock market crash, said, 'Bull markets are born on pessimism, grow on scepticism, mature on optimism and die on euphoria.'

Look at charts

A picture tells a thousand words and a share price graph gives an instant overview of a company's investment profile. Manipulated over varying lengths of time and compared to other benchmarks (such as pan-market indexes and other similar companies' share price performances), charts provide invaluable research short cuts. If the charts show a sudden share price drop, you are immediately prompted to investigate what caused the movement. If there are lots of precipitous shifts, you may well conclude that investment is risky as well as volatile.

Some think that the patterns made by lines on a chart can be used to make predictions about future price movements. The talk of so-called 'chartists' or 'technical analysts' is full of phrases such as 'double tops', 'levels of resistance', 'saucers', 'Spanish castles' and 'golden crosses'. While sober analysis suggests there is some truth in the techniques, there is also much hooey spoken on the subject. For many, the skills of a chartist are akin to the talents of a palm reader.

Overall, charts provide a useful tool of analysis but should be expected to provide no more than sketchy insights as to what might happen in future.

Investment manias are a fact of life

Niall Ferguson, the historian, writing in his 2008 book *The Ascent of Money*, said, 'So long as human expectations of the future veer from the over-optimistic to the over-pessimistic – from greed to fear – stock prices will tend to trace an erratic path.'

The Dutch mania for tulips, observed in the 1640s, shows how misplaced sentiment can drive price shifts that are as dangerous as they are striking. In 1636 twelve acres of building land were exchanged for a red and white flowering bulb called – rather ironically, if you think about the meaning of its name – *Semper Augustus*. The craze spun hopelessly out of control and the price was shown, eventually, to be ridiculous.

Just as the factual backing for investment booms is often shown to be wildly exaggerated, the fundamental reasons for a downturn can be magnified. The bursting of investment bubbles often leads to periods of depression, just as investment euphoria gets out of hand. The most memorable stock market depression came in the 1930s, when President Franklin D. Roosevelt was prompted to tell the American people, in 1932, 'The only thing we have to fear is fear itself.'

Financial market manias may come around less often if modern investors have more understanding of them. However, investors are better served if they assume manias will always occur, then try not to get caught by them. Some investors work on the 'greater fool' theory – that is, the theory that they will make money from baseless manias because they will be able to find a buyer who is even more foolish than they are themselves who will be taken in for longer. Some of the Dutch tulip traders may have been fully aware of the nonsense that was unfolding but saw the opportunity to trade on the sentimental flaws of fellow citizens.

No doubt some make money on this basis. But plenty more will be caught out and find themselves holding duds when the music stops.

Be prepared to buck the trend

It is sometimes – although not invariably – right to go against instinct. It is sometimes right to give credence to counterfactual evidence and act against the wisdom (such as it is) of the crowd. Elaine Garzarelli, a Wall Street analyst who won fame for anticipating the 1987 stock market crash, said, 'I do the opposite to what I feel I should do. When I'm sick in my stomach, it's time to buy. When I feel great, it's time to sell.'

Just as it is often appropriate to go with the flow, there is a time to swim against the tide.

There is a time to act, and a time to be inactive

Like a fine wine or a malt whisky, investments often need time to mature. Yes, good investors are quick-witted and nimble; but they are also patient, thick-skinned and willing to show confidence in the wisdom of their long-term decision-making. Benjamin Graham, a godfather of so-called 'value' investing – that is, investing which seeks out enduring value in stocks – said, 'Short term, the stock market is a voting machine. Long term, it's a weighing machine.'

Activity, on the other hand, can be seen as a sign of weakness or failure because it may indicate the need to correct mistakes. If your financial adviser or investment manager is overactive it may be a sign of mediocrity – and since activity provides an excuse to levy fees, mediocrity can come at added cost.

Cramer's Law

Jim Cramer is the journalist who founded thestreet.
com and won wide notoriety for his *Mad Money*
tirade on CNBC against Federal Reserve chairman
Ben Bernanke, and others, in August 2007. He said,
'I am neither a bear nor a bull. I am an agnostic
opportunist. I want to make money short- and long-
term. I want to find good situations and exploit
them.'

Sound long-term investment enables people to
live more comfortably, with more confidence that
they will enjoy satisfactory living standards. But
short-term gains are gains as well and the creed of
long-termism can be a smokescreen for prevarication
or an excuse for poor performance. Besides, if you
get the short-term decisions right, things are likely to
work out for the best in the long term. Take care of
the pennies and cents and the pounds, dollars and
euros will take care of themselves.

The misleading theory of relativity

It is easy to take comfort from the fact that, while your investments have performed poorly, they have not done as badly as some others in the market as a whole. It is also easy to feel bad if your investments rise in value, but not as far or fast as those of peers. It is far more important to achieve positive returns, in absolute terms, as frequently and regularly as possible – whatever the wider market conditions. If your investments rise in value and run ahead of the rate of inflation, the job is done irrespective of the relative performance picture.

Always leave something for the market

Good investors know there will, almost always, be people who are braver, luckier and/or more foolish than themselves. Sound investors appreciate the sense of leaving before the end of a party, the danger of outstaying their welcome and the ease with which one can miss the last bus out of the good times.

Don't look for entertainment, look for profit

Paul Samuelson, the Nobel Prize-winning economist, said, 'Investing should be more like watching paint dry or watching grass grow. If you want excitement, take $800 and go to Las Vegas.'

By and large, investment is work, not leisure. Like dieting, finance and investment are a challenge and are satisfying if successful. But they are a means to an end, not an end in themselves.

Look past the gimmicks

Freebies, such as air miles, or spurious association with famous golfers or pop stars are a dangerous distraction. Focus all your attention on the stuff that really matters: the hard facts and the tough choices.

The nightclub rule

The building of an investment portfolio requires discipline. Once you have a mature portfolio of investments, the nightclub rule helps you to exercise control. Like the bouncer on the door of a popular nightclub, let one in when one has come out. Introducing a new investment only when you have sold one makes you ask hard questions about which investment candidates have the best prospects. It also leads to regular examination of when, or if, it is best to sell.

Don't let tax tales wag investment dogs

Tax breaks are meaningless if the underlying investment is poor.

It is, of course, only natural to want to avoid paying tax, because it is a cost that drags on investment performance Effective, legal tax avoidance enhances investment returns in an environment where there are precious few certainties and it is only sensible to use all available tax shelters. In Britain, Personal Equity Plans (PEPs), Tax Exempt Special Savings Accounts (TESSAs) and Individual Savings Accounts (ISAs) have all played valuable roles. In the United States, the so-called '401k' schemes are popular, and rightly so, because they relieve the burdens of tax.

But in many ways it is a good sign if you pay tax, because it shows you are making profits. Investment history is littered with examples of investors who chased the tax break and forgot the importance of making money in the first place. In Britain in 1988, property prices spiralled upwards ahead of a change that reined in the tax breaks available to residential mortgage holders. Couples, and many less than well-acquainted people, rushed to buy together before the deadline. The rush led to an increase in the price of houses that was reversed once the tax change had come into force. Personal relationships were ruined too as folk marched themselves into cohabitation before they were ready for it.

LAWS OF FINANCE

It is important to grasp some of the underlying principles of finance. Context and proper understanding are vital if you are going to make money and avoid losses. At root, these usually add up to simple common sense.

Look at the big picture

Investors, especially personal investors, often ignore large parts of the big economic picture. To a certain extent, this is because it is difficult to understand and frustrating because there are few hard-and-fast answers to questions raised. Many investors prefer to focus attention on specific issues that seem likely to affect individual shares, or on narrow comparisons such as the difference between the interest rates payable on deposits at rival banks. It is as if investors assume they can do nothing to take account of the big picture and are somehow obliged to assume – or hope – that the general environment will be benign. Should investors ignore the macro-risks? Of course not.

Most wealth comes from income

It is tempting to assume that investments have innate capital value. In fact, the value of most things is related, directly or indirectly, to the income produced.

Think about the value of a piece of low-grade farmland. Imagine how for years it was good for nothing but grazing sheep. The capital value of this land would be directly related to the price of wool or mutton. If the income from wool or mutton was low, the capital value of the land would also be low. Now think what would happen to the value of the land if it was laid out as a golf course. If the golf course was popular and could sustain a flow of green fees higher than the price of wool or mutton, the capital value of the land would increase.

Now think about what would happen if economic or social circumstances took a turn. If changes in financial realities, or fashion, meant that no one wanted to play golf, the value of keeping sheep on the land would be reasserted. The value of mutton or wool might increase if economic conditions got really bad and that would make the land worth more than it was the last time it was given over to grazing. Value is inextricably linked to income.

The golden goose protocol

The goose that lays the golden eggs has minimal value as a carcass; it has much greater value as a producer of precious metal. Moreover, if you can calculate how many eggs will come, their size and the prevailing price of gold when they are laid, you will get a pretty good idea of the present value of the living goose.

Value equals the sum of future income. In finance and investment, so-called 'discounted cash flow' (DCF) sums are used to calculate present value of future earnings. Using this method, it is assumed that 'cash' (another word for profit, in this context) will 'flow' to the owner. If you know what the cash flow will be, you will have a good idea what to pay for the right to collect it. If Cole Enterprises generates £100 of income for the next five years, Cole Enterprises is worth £500.

In practice, sadly, the sums are more complicated. Cash flows change over time. They may go up and they may go down; they may do both and it is devilishly difficult to make accurate forecasts either way. No one can be sure of the appropriate timescales either. Will Cole Enterprises be around for ever? Or will it run out of steam in five, ten or twenty-five years' time? Inflation is another headache. You also need to factor in what you might earn in a risk-free, or almost risk-free, environment. It is because of this litany of doubts that cash flow estimates must be reduced, or 'discounted', to take account of the risks that the income will be miscalculated, interrupted or eroded by inflation. Spreadsheets are an invaluable tool in arriving at answers. Ready-made DCF calculators are available on the Internet.

It is common, and sensible, to see dividend income as a proxy for cash flow. The capital value of shares is certainly closely related to the dividend income paid out. It is no easy task, but if investors can work out what dividends a company will pay in future they can gain good insight into the capital value of the enterprise.

Dividends are crucial

Nils Taube, a well-respected late-twentieth-century investment professional, said, 'Do not underestimate the value of a company with a strong record of paying an increasing dividend. The long-term evidence suggests that dividends have accounted for an astonishing two-thirds of investors' total returns.'

Dividends seem, at first sight, insignificantly small. How can a few pennies or dimes matter much? Yet thanks in part to the wonders of compound interest, and the fact that successful companies increase dividends at an accelerating pace, dividends create lots of value. The best companies, arguably, are the ones that can increase dividend payments, because if dividend payments rise the capital value of a company tends to rise.

The law of compound interest

Some of the best, most reliable investment returns come to those who are prepared to wait. Charlie Munger, Warren Buffett's business partner, said, 'There are huge mathematical advantages to doing nothing.' Interest – or income of another sort – obviously swells the value of a lump sum. Less obvious is that interest paid on interest magnifies the value of investments, and increases exponentially. Like a snowball rolling down a hill, value can be added at exponential rates. After a surprisingly short period the accrued interest can grow larger than the original lump of capital.

The three unwritten laws of debt: it's good, it's bad and it can get ugly

---

The key to telling the difference between good, bad and ugly debt is to understand the full costs, to make sober estimates of your ability to repay and to judge the likely future value of assets or services bought.

The Good. The essential debt question is a simple one: will the value of my purchase grow faster than the cost of the debt I take on to make the acquisition? As long as the investment profits come, and are greater than the interest costs, borrowing works well.

One of the simplest ways to pump up investment returns is to borrow. Say you have £100 and expect to make 10 per cent a year. If you only invest the £100 you will make £10 profit, ending up with £110. If you borrow an additional £100, invest the £200 at 10 per cent a year you will make returns of £20 in twelve months. Even if you expect to pay £5 in interest, as long as you repay the £100 loan promptly you will make £15 instead of £10 profit on the original £100. That is a big deal – a 50 per cent improvement.

Debt can be a force for good. Ask the desperately poor women of Bangladesh who have improved their lives, and the lives of their families, by borrowing tiny amounts of money from their neighbours in schemes dreamed up by Mohammed Yunus, the Nobel Prize-winning proponent of micro-finance. There is great value in education, for example, and if the only route to higher knowledge comes through borrowing, it may well be justified. Better education often leads to better jobs and better salaries too, so borrowing for education may also make sound financial sense. Debt is good in the sense that it buys time: purchases that would otherwise be impossible – most importantly, perhaps, a place to live – can be brought forward.

The Bad. Debt brings costs – financial and moral – which are easy to underestimate and tempting to ignore. Moreover, as Polonius says in *Hamlet*, borrowing 'dulls the edge of husbandry'.

It is easy for honest borrowers to become enslaved

in a repayment process which, thanks to the burdens of interest, chains people to an exhausting treadmill. Even relatively modest rates of interest rack up the overall costs if you borrow over any significant length of time. For example, if you borrow £150,000 to buy a house over twenty-five years at 6 per cent, the total cost of a loan, in capital repayments and interest, is about £290,000. That is nearly double the original loan. At 12 per cent a year, the cost of repaying a twenty-five-year loan is more than trebled.

The Ugly. Down the centuries, attitudes towards debt have been overwhelmingly ones of concern, dread and opprobrium. From the biblical writer of the Book of Proverbs ('The rich ruleth over the poor, and the borrower is servant to the lender'), to Publius Syrus, the first-century Roman author, who said, 'Debt is the slavery of the free', to Ogden Nash, the American writer, who said, 'Some debts are fun when you are acquiring them, but none are fun when you set about retiring them', the underlying sentiments are fear and loathing.

Imprudent indebtedness lies at the heart of many, if not the majority of, investment failures. Fraud, silliness and bad luck account for most of the rest. If you make investment losses on borrowed money, the effect is crippling. Say you lose 10 per cent on investments bolstered by borrowing on a scale mentioned above, £200 will become £180, and with the interest bill that will fall to £175. Repay the debt and you are left with only £75. Because of the debt, a 10 per cent slip in the underlying value of an investment is translated into losses of 25 per cent.

Those who borrow run the real risk of bankruptcy, and may end up with less than nothing, while those who do not borrow are likely to 'merely' run the risk of seeing their wealth shrink. Institutional investment funds such as the LCTM hedge fund that went bust in 1998 do not stop at borrowing £100 for every £100 of capital they have. LTCM borrowed £2,000 for every £100 of capital. As long as the investment judgements paid off, LTCM retained something akin to a licence to print money. Once the judgements went off the rails, however, it was not just LTCM that found itself in trouble. With leverage this large, investment had only to decline 5 per cent to cause complete wipeout. Moreover, as the losses climbed further, the problem then transferred to those who lent to LTCM.

When it comes to debt, governments have a reputation which is no less ugly. 'The practice of contracting debt,' said David Hume, the Scottish philosopher, 'will almost infallibly be abused in every government. It would scarcely be more imprudent to give a prodigal son a credit in every banker's shop in London, than to empower a statesman to draw bills, in this manner, upon posterity.'

Finance is brainy

James Surowiecki wrote, 'What is the free market? It's a mechanism designed to solve a coordination problem, arguably the most important coordination problem: getting resources to the right places at the right cost.'

Investment involves the provision of finance to people, in companies and governments, who, mostly and indirectly, seek economic and social progress. The financial system exists to facilitate exchange between those who want money and those who have it. When money passes from an investor to a government or a company, a 'primary market transaction' is said to have taken place. Subsequently, shares or bonds issued in a primary move are traded between different investors in 'secondary market transactions'. This 'second-hand' market is essential because it allows investors to cash in their investment without obliging government or companies to liquidate. A thriving second-hand market also gives important indicators as to what is thought good, and bad, use of capital. The price of second-hand capital put to good use is high, while the second-hand price of squandered capital falls.

Free markets are far from perfect – as frequent crises of financial confidence and competence testify. But the mid- to late-twentieth-century history of communist China, the Soviet Union and left-leaning developing nations in Africa indicates just how poor governments can be at allocating and distributing capital to worthwhile causes.

Finance and investment provide a vibrant mechanism for supplying capital to where it is needed and economic history books present convincing evidence that open markets allow more people to live more comfortable, more rewarding and healthier lives. It is not for nothing that pro-market thinkers sometimes call finance 'the brain of the economy' and believe the brain works best when it is given plenty of freedom.

The law of diminishing returns

Investors are attracted to assets offering high returns, but if an asset, or an investment project, is swamped by capital it usually follows that returns will be diluted. In extreme cases, torrents of capital – coming and going – can destabilise or undermine the investment prospects of even the finest ideas. Imagine, for instance, that the price of copper rises. If it does, mining companies will be tempted to spend on exploring for new mines. But money spent on investment will increase supplies of copper and, eventually, reduce the price of the metal. In this context, personal investors may note the danger of being sucked into investment markets shot through with optimism. The evidence of rising prices is comforting, but past success reduces the room for future growth.

The civilising law of finance

Money is an essential component of civilisation – albeit that civilisations have not always shown themselves to be civilised. In some senses money almost defines civilisation. Why? Before settled civilisations were created, men were nomads, hunters and gatherers, jacks of all trades. Cavemen subsisted, making or taking from nature everything they wanted or needed. They had no need of money.

As settled communities emerged, people became

more efficient, productive and affluent. Instead of hunting and gathering, people took specialised roles as farmers or bread makers (and then clothes designers and rocket scientists). Specialisation meant people got better at what they did and had more opportunities to make discoveries, to invent new techniques and to explore fresh opportunities. But without money settled civilisations could not function. Without money there would be no effective way for specialists to exchange the things they make with the numerous other things they need but do not, or cannot, make themselves.

Money oils the cogs of civilisation, of specialisation, of progress and of human ingenuity. It is because of money that the people of the world can give their resources, strength, skills and time to others and it is thanks to currencies that people enjoy enhanced health and more everyday comforts.

Money is moral

Finance is often thought to be *amoral*, perhaps because it often seems to cause *immoral* behaviour. In fact, issues of morality – or ethics – cannot and should not be divorced from money. Investors may argue long and hard about the precise nature of ethics, but the rule of thumb must be that unethical behaviour creates bad investments. Sustained investment profits arise from companies and financial institutions that perform useful social functions.

'There can be no high civility without a deep morality,' said Ralph Waldo Emerson, the American essayist.

Inflation is deadly

Ronald Reagan, the former US president who led his country at a time of high inflation and put its defeat near the top of his political agenda, said, 'Inflation is as violent as a mugger, as frightening as an armed robber and as deadly as a hit man.' Along with generating income, one of the most basic reasons to invest is to ensure that nest eggs retain real value amid the rising cost of living.

Inflation is a wolf dressed as a sheep

Inflation is calculated by totting up the total cost of a basket of everyday goods and services and measuring the change, usually over the period of a year. It is sometimes referred to in terms of the 'cost of living' or the RPI.

Inflation is especially dangerous because in the short term it appears to be a good thing. Superficially, rising prices might appear helpful. They look good for wage earners because employers are obliged to increase salaries. Inflation appears positive for industrialists too, since they can put up prices and increase revenues. Inflation also appeals to borrowers, including mortgage payers and governments, because it reduces the size of debts in real terms. How? If incomes rise and debt interest payments stay the same, borrowing burdens get lighter.

But although inflation may appear harmless enough, it lowers the underlying value of money and makes it more difficult to plan ahead. Wage earners might get paid more, but they also have to pay more for the things they need and want. Industrialists also have to pay more to produce goods. Since lenders lose where borrowers gain, inflation makes it more difficult to take out loans which, used sensibly, help people improve their lives.

Milton Friedman, the free market economist, said, 'Inflation is the one form of taxation that can be imposed without legislation.' Why? Tax reduces spending directly; inflation means people can buy less stuff. In essence, they add up to the same thing.

Inflation can even reward imprudent borrowers, because they may escape the painful results of their foolishness. Indirectly, therefore, inflation can breed foolish economic behaviour.

Even low inflation can be highly damaging

As is shown by rare but significant examples, from Weimar Germany to modern-day Zimbabwe, hyper-inflation can take away everything, then spark civil or social unrest. Small amounts of inflation do lots of damage as well. If you retire on a fixed income and the cost of living rises even quite slowly, the things that you can put in your shopping basket will become progressively less appetising. They may become progressively less nutritious too.

In 1966, the year England won the soccer World Cup, you would have paid £7.50 for a basket of goods that cost a total of £100 forty years later. In the twenty-five years after Ronald Reagan became president of the United States of America the cost of a shopping basket more than doubled. Even over the ten years between 1995 and 2005, when annual inflation rates were low enough to be almost forgotten about, prices rose nearly 30 per cent in all.

In trust we trust

'Glass, china, and reputation are easily cracked, and never well mended,' said American statesman Benjamin Franklin.

Why do people repay debts? Is it because they feel morally obliged? Is it because they fear retribution, as lenders carry out threats to repossess goods or inflict injury when debts are left unpaid? Do people fear the actions of bailiffs or the due process of law? Feelings of duty to lenders exist, oddly enough, even when rates of interest are usuriously high.

Part of the obligation comes because people do as they would be done by. A borrower might not renege on a promise for fear that he or she might later be a lender and be hoisted by the same petard. Borrowers also know that if they renege on a debt they will find it more difficult to borrow in future. It is very likely to be more expensive. It may not be possible to find anyone willing to lend to a blacklisted borrower.

Those who provide capital to companies and governments may have some contractual security offered in exchange, but in the final analysis investors have to trust those executives and ministers who take the money. They trust them to make wise choices, to invest honestly and prudently, to pay interest and dividends, and to stand by obligations to protect, and enhance, the value of savings.

Trust lies at the heart of finance – ancient and modern – although it is, perhaps, for entirely selfish reasons that users of capital try hard not to betray investors' trust. The financial world is held together by a wide and intricate web of promises.

The rules of global engagement

People, and nations, often seek self-sufficiency because they do not want to depend on others. The popularity of free trade varies from era to era, but globalisation comes about as the movement of goods, services, people and capital becomes less and less encumbered.

Detractors believe that free markets give big business participants carte blanche to take unfair advantage of poorer and less powerful people. People in rich nations, for instance, can get their shoes made more cheaply by labourers in poor countries who are obliged to accept lower wages – and more harmful working conditions. In the process, it is said, captains of industry pocket huge wealth for themselves. Free markets, detractors say, are inadequately regulated for the common good, and people and products are homogenised. They say that ethics suffer and environmental imperatives are ignored.

Supporters of free trade, on the other hand,

contend that free markets create wealth in such massive quantity that it offers more than adequate compensation for the disadvantages. Globalisation, say supporters, allows different people in different parts of the world to play to their strengths and, in doing so, make steady gains in their standards of living. (This is the economic law of 'comparative advantage'.) By joining a global community of specialists – be they expert in making cheap running shoes or expensive nuclear reactors – people across the globe benefit from the higher-class effort of fellow citizens of the world. Meanwhile the faults of free trade, supporters say, come because the principles of openness and transparency are misunderstood, neglected or abused.

Investors are obliged to consider the global nature of investment. Since so many companies operate multinationally, a listing on one stock exchange – be it New York or Mumbai, Hong Kong or Amsterdam – will depend, at least to an extent, on things that happen way beyond that city's walls and across national borders.

Foreign exchange is a law unto itself

One way to look at currencies is as displaying the 'price' of a national economy. Currencies will fall in value if there are more sellers than buyers and they will rise if there are more buyers than sellers. If international investors think the economy is strong, the currency will be highly priced. If the global investment community dislikes a country's finances and its capacity to do business, the currency will be weak.

The underlying realities are enormously complex and shifts in the world's foreign exchange market defy ready explanations. Conscious that exchange rates exert enormous influence on the economic welfare of nations, many governments have tried hard to control exchange rates. Hence the effort spent on maintaining the gold standard, the Bretton Woods agreement and, more recently, the development of the euro. That said, many other governments, scarred by the cost of failure, have concluded that currencies are too difficult to manage and best left to their own devices.

Those who invest purely on movements in the foreign exchange market can become fabulously wealthy and hindsight can make their investment strategies look easy. Yet currencies are so unpredictable that many investors try to ignore them. The sensible option is to ensure that any exposure is hedged – or insured against. If nothing else, you should ensure that you hold assets in the currency that you are likely to want to spend, because that way you are insulated from shifting exchange rates.

It is best to avoid the currencies of smaller or underdeveloped countries and, if any exposure is thought necessary, to build balanced positions in several of the larger ones.

The flawed law of perfect markets

Many economic theories are based on an assumption that markets work perfectly, bowing to the Efficient Market Hypothesis. Market participants, it is said, are always familiar with all available information and they act quickly, in an economically rational way. Perfect market theorists also assume that investors have access to all the capital they need to fund whatever it is they wish to do.

The ideal market operator is the figuratively named *Homo economicus*. In practice, perfect market conditions exist only in the largest, most frequently used markets, and even then their existence is a matter of intense debate among economists. The key for amateur investors, who may be tempted to analyse investments in the context of their own idealised parameters, is to be aware that any textbook-style theory needs to be adjusted to take account of real-world conditions and real-life circumstances.

When video recorders began to appear in the

1980s, Betamax technology was widely acclaimed as being superior to VHS. Consumers – against what is widely assumed to be better judgements – sometimes choose to follow the less perfect route. Investors, therefore, must sometimes bend to consumers' illogical or irrational ways and back things that appear, in theory or practice, less good.

Sound finance is built on fairness

'Fair exchange,' as the proverb goes, 'is no robbery.'

In popular imagination finance polarises society. It separates rich and poor, creating divisions between the 'haves' and the 'have nots' (and, it is sometimes said, the 'have yachts'). Experience suggests these weaknesses are both real and endemic: one has only to recall the United Nations research that suggests the richest 2 per cent of the world's population own half the world's household wealth, while the poorest 50 per cent of the global population control just 1 per cent of the world's riches.

Yet sound financial systems are based on extending fairness, and equality, and distributing wealth. Reliability and sustainability come through linking diverse groups in mutual financial interest. Take employer-run pension schemes, for example. Through pension schemes, employers and employees, shareholders, regulators, taxpayers, customers and retired people are bound by the common interest of creating and sustaining long-term wealth. Each stakeholder has an invaluable role to play.

Private pension schemes, of the sort developed in Europe and North America in the twentieth century, have thrived in large part because they connected owners and users of investment capital, employers and employees, consumers, producers, taxpayers and the beneficiaries of social welfare in an intricate, sturdy, symbiotic financial network.

In such delicate economic 'ecosystems', if one or other group becomes too strong or too weak, the whole intricately symbiotic relationship breaks down. In the UK in the 1970s, the trade unions held the upper hand and, arguably at least, destabilised the economy because they held too much influence. In the early to mid-part of the 2000s, the interests of financial capital held sway in a way that proved far from healthy.

It is easy to argue that company executives grabbed too much power and the ordinary investors (who ultimately own most of the capital used by companies) enjoyed too little influence. This might, perhaps should, prompt private investors to take a more active role in the management of their money and the companies in which it is invested.

It is important to watch for companies where one or other set of stakeholders stands out. The over-mighty power of directors and employees of the Enron electricity trading charabanc may, ultimately, be why that story ended in disaster. Robert Maxwell's publishing empire imploded partly because Robert Maxwell's interest held precedence over all others. The interests of other stakeholders, especially the pensioners, were neglected, with disastrous consequences.

Mind your own business

Investment frequently works on the pursuit of self-interest. This is commonly seen as a bad thing; but self-motivation, and self-preservation, are powerful agents of action which help enhance wealth and living standards. The contrast between home-ownership and renting illustrates the point. Compared to those who rent, those who own their homes tend to take greater responsibility for the upkeep of the fabric and the fittings. They are more likely to invest in the property to improve it. Neighbourhoods where owner-occupiers predominate tend to be more contented places than areas where renting is prevalent – although many other factors, especially wealth, exert significant influence too.

Meanwhile, if those who can take care of themselves do take care of themselves, less fortunate members of society may benefit from more concentrated campaigns of philanthropic assistance. If individuals in markets create wealth by pursuing their own self-interest they can be taxed in ways that provide common goods. Charitable ambitions may be best met using profits from markets, not by expecting market forces to achieve success directly. Governments and other civic authorities have a critical role to play in planning, regulating and providing welfare services. Where possible, however, individuals are well placed (and probably better placed) to provide for themselves.

Investors are well advised to ensure that they look after number one.

SECTION SIX

AXIOMS OF EXPERIENCE

Any fool can invest, but a fool and his or her money are also easily parted. Although we need to be careful when we look backwards, history provides the only factual information available to investors. Results improve with knowledge, application and experience. 'We shall not grow wiser before we learn that much that we have done was very foolish,' said Friedrich August von Hayek, the Austrian economic philosopher.

Investment history repeats itself

Sir John Templeton said, 'The four most expensive words in the English language are, "This time it's different."'

There are three ways to get rich

You can steal, you can get lucky or you can do it the hard and slow way, by working.

It is the third route that provides the surest path to financial comfort for most people. You may find yourself having to work hard to maintain or increase the value of your wealth in an acceptable fashion, but if you want a clear conscience you have to put your intelligence, skills, muscle-power and time into harness.

Opportunity knocks

Louis L'Amour, the American adventure story writer, said, 'Some say opportunity knocks only once. That is not true. Opportunity knocks all the time, but you have to be ready for it.'

Proper planning prevents poor practice

Investment insight comes with information and intelligence. Those armed with facts and astute interpretative skills are best placed to protect and improve the value of their savings. In the last paragraph of the first chapter of *Pride and Prejudice*, Jane Austen describes Mrs Bennet as a woman of 'mean understanding, little information, and uncertain temper'. The three attributes are connected and, with finance and investment, often lead to disaster.

Playing games helps

You can acquire knowledge and develop investment instincts through simulations and trials. By playing, the cost of making mistakes can also be reduced. Run dummy portfolios using web tools offered by online stockbroking firms.

Important principles of risk-taking and investment can be learned through board games such as backgammon and chess, or playing card games such as poker and, especially, contract bridge. Lord George, the former Governor of the Bank of England, used to keep his financial antennae tuned by playing cards.

Investment wisdom must be appropriately applied

Good investors know the importance of patience and accept that the field is underpinned by enduring truths. They also appreciate that things change. That which is appropriate for a twenty-five-year-old just embarking on the world of work is not right for a seventy-five-year-old pensioner. It is sometimes said that one's age determines the percentage split of a portfolio between higher-risk equities and lower-risk bonds. Aged twenty, it is said, you ought to have 20 per cent in bonds, because the better long-term returns come from equities. At eighty, bonds should account for 80 per cent, because older people are less well placed to shoulder the risk in equities as they can be less sure that wounded equities portfolios will be healed by the passage of time. The wisdom of the 'age–percentage rule' is open to debate. It is unarguable, however, that differing personal circumstances demand that different investment strategies are deployed.

Choose horses for courses

Different sorts of investment wisdom should be applied in different market circumstances. Just as young investors will make different judgements from older ones, investment strategies suited to an era of low inflation may not work in an era of high inflation. Similarly, your investment choices may be influenced by purpose. What suits the parent saving to help pay for a child's education, for instance, will not suit the teenager saving for a new computer game or the newlyweds who want to buy their first house.

The law of unintended consequences

Good investors, as well as sound policymakers, entrepreneurs, captains of industry, professional advisers, bankers, employees and consumers, know the difference between theory and practice. All sorts of stuff, sometimes called 'noise', gets in the way. Some factors are foreseeable, but many aren't. Some things are avoidable and plans must often be altered out of necessity.

Consider the example of the children's nursery which found itself stuck with children past going-home time, as some parents and carers failed to turn up at the appointed hour. The nursery instituted a system of fines, hoping to re-establish punctuality, but instead of curing the problem, things got worse. Instead of seeing the charge levied as a fine, as was intended, parents and carers viewed the fine as a fee, giving them licence to run late.

Any decision may have an unintended consequence, of course, and unchecked fears of the unknown can lead to debilitating inactivity. The key is to think creatively about what the unintended consequences might be.

The love of money is the root of all evil

Money, according to the old saw, is at the root of all evil. It is surely more accurate to say that people are at the root of all evil, and their evil is often, but not always, expressed in the way they handle matters financial. It may be better to think of money as neutral, as a utility the character of which changes according to the people who use it and the way it is used.

Accurately quoted from the Bible, where it appears in the First Book of Timothy, the phrase is rather different. 'The love of money,' writes the author, 'is the root of all evil.'

Keep it commercial

There is an Arabian proverb which says, 'Live together like brothers and do business like strangers.' Human emotion cannot be removed from investment and finance because investment and finance are, ultimately, human, but it is preferable to operate with calm detachment. Benjamin Graham, the US investor whose 1949 book *The Intelligent Investor* was described by Warren Buffett as 'by far the best book about investing ever written', said, 'Investment is most intelligent when it is most businesslike.'

Money can't buy you love

Good investors avoid becoming emotionally attached to their investments because they know their affections will not be reciprocated. Nor is it wise to stick with an investment for sentimental or irrational reasons, out of misplaced loyalty or because of past associations.

Although generosity is beguiling, and lavishness assists those who act out impressions of affection, money cannot buy love. The best to hope for was outlined by the British comedian Spike Milligan, who said, 'Money can't buy you happiness, but it does bring you a more pleasant form of misery.'

Trick or trite?

Consumer guides to finance are often little more than thinly disguised marketing exercises designed to encourage readers to hand over large lumps of cash to financial advisers, investment managers, companies or governments. Alternatively, and sometimes simultaneously, the literature is patronising. (This book, it is hoped, is neither.) Better information is presented in a neutral and factual way where the inevitable uncertainties of investment are clearly outlined. Company reports, since they are usually written by executives who are trying to impress their owners (and paymasters), invariably stress the positives and brush harsher realities under the carpet. Investors need to adjust their judgements accordingly.

There is no magic wand

It is tempting to hope that easy solutions can be found to big problems. Untold riches do come to lazy people at minimal outlay, but only when they shoulder the almost unbelievable risk of 'investing' in lotteries. In the real world there are no silver bullets and the mundane often takes precedence over the magical.

Novelty has little value

The best 'new' ideas are reformulations of tried and tested schemes. In 1997 the UK's new Labour government introduced tax-exempt investment schemes called Individual Savings Accounts (ISAs) at the same time as withdrawing Personal Equity Plans (PEPs). There are some differences between the two, but the similarities are far more significant than the differences. Neither was an investment as such, so much as a government-sponsored tax break. ISAs were not a bad idea, but neither were they new.

Similarly, the relatively young Nasdaq US stock exchange attracted attention and plaudits, especially in the late 1990s, because it was identified as the stock market where shares in new, exciting growth companies were traded. Microsoft, for instance, was the Nasdaq's pin-up. Later it was Google's turn. This is not to suggest there is anything intrinsically wrong with Nasdaq – the competition it posed for the New York stock exchange enhanced service standards all round – but the novelty factor, of Nasdaq and its shares, may have led investors to ascribe some spurious value to the shares. The inherent qualities of companies, rather than the branding of a particular stock exchange platform, should drive valuations and investment activity.

It is often better to buy second-hand because prices are tested against the wisdom of the many market participants. The value of new shares is not tested – or not thoroughly tested – against the rough and tumble of market activity. The value of new shares may be determined more by the dreams of an egotistical chief executive or an investment banker whose fees rise in step with the price at which new shares are sold.

Be afraid, be very afraid

John MacKay of the Toronto General Trusts, writing a new foreword in 1914 to Andrew Dickson Wright's

1912 book *Fiat Money Inflation in France: How It Came, What It Brought, and How It Ended*, said, 'Legislatures are as powerless to abrogate moral and economic laws as they are to abrogate physical laws. They cannot convert wrong into right nor divorce effect from cause, either by parliamentary majorities, or by unity of supporting opinions. The penalties of such legislative folly will always be exacted in inexorable time.'

Right or wrong, investors find it hard to trust politicians and are sceptical of the power of regulation. They fear that governments and regulators add cost, and hassle, to the activities of corporations and to the process of investment. The power of the political process is also subject to suspicion. On some occasions politics can have a rapid and significant impact. As often, if not more often, politicians are less powerful than economic forces. It was P. J. O'Rourke, the American satirist, who said, 'When buying and selling are controlled by legislation, the first things to be bought and sold are legislators.'

Hayek's law

Playing Lawrence Garfield in the 1991 film *Other People's Money*, Danny DeVito, the actor, said, 'There's only one thing I love more than money. You know what that is? Other people's money.' Just as fools and money are easily parted, so it is easy to spend other people's money foolishly. The law should prompt investors to keep company directors – who are the employees of shareholders – under close scrutiny and subject to best practices of corporate governance. Investors may find this law especially informative when assessing whether government ministers and officials are best placed to spend citizens' money.

Most of all, this law should prompt investors to question the actions of investment advisers. Some degree of detachment can be useful, but it is far easier to experiment with money that is not your own and fail to spot extravagance, profligacy, wastage and fuzzy logic. Be happy to accept full responsibility for the investment decisions that affect your savings. At the very least, it is good to ensure that those looking after your cash have what is sometimes called 'skin in the game'.

Leaning heavily on the thoughts of Friedrich Hayek, Dick Amey, a US Republican politician who led the House of Representatives from 1995 to 2003, said, 'Three groups spend other people's money: children, thieves, politicians. All three need supervision.'

Don't forget the admin

Elihu Root, US Secretary of State to Theodore Roosevelt and recipient of the 1912 Nobel Peace Prize, said, 'The worst, the hardest, the most disagreeable thing that you may have to do may be the thing that counts most, because it is the hard discipline, and it alone, that makes possible the highest efficiency.'

Sound and efficient administration is important

because it makes tiresome chores, such as filing tax returns, easier. Efficiency reduces costs – in terms of time or money – and, most importantly of all, it leads to improved practice. If you know, quite precisely, how much you pay in share dealing fees you will know, quite precisely, whether it is cost-effective to trade in individual shares. If you keep the paperwork well organised, you are also likely to give your investment thinking logical structure. Good record keeping allows easy access to reminders of the things you have done in the past. In this way you learn from mistakes and can repeat winning formulae.

Gosh, it is dull, and because it is dull it is difficult. Yet it is also essential.

History needs context

It is necessary to use lessons of the past carefully, as it is easy to draw parallels where none exists. Good decisions come because wise people remember the past, analyse the present and look to the future, but good decisions are also singular. They are suited only to one particular set of circumstances and while some different circumstances may appear similar, each is unique, even if only because it is taking place at a different point in time. Finance and investment must be handled with ever-adapting dexterity. As the Greek philosopher Heraclitus, writing 2,500 years ago, said, 'You can't step into the same river twice.'

Look to the future

It is sometimes said that to make an investment decision based entirely on past performance is like driving a car using only the rear-view mirror. The adage belittles the importance of history and ignores the fact that past performance provides some of the only hard facts about an investment. However, it is necessary to look forward, and remember there is no certainty that past performance – good or bad – will be repeated.

Honesty is the best policy

The benefits of transparency are encapsulated by the aphorism attributed to Louis Brandeis, the US Supreme Court Justice who had a hand in the establishment of the Federal Reserve, the US central bank and the Federal Trade Commission: 'Sunshine is the best disinfectant.'

Individuals need to be honest with themselves – in the light of fresh information, for instance. The most sustainable investments are ones that are grounded in honesty, and the existence of a genuine and wholesome need which can be honestly satisfied.

Rules are made to be broken

'You cannot make yourself feel something you do not feel, but you can make yourself do right in spite of your feelings,' said Pearl S. Buck, the American winner of the 1938 Nobel Prize for Literature.

In finance and investment, as in life, there are very few absolute truths. Hard-and-fast laws are often attractive because blind obedience is effortless, but even sensible rules are not always applicable or appropriate, and have downsides. Hence the value of the Chinese proverb which says that deep wisdom comes with deep doubts.

Although certainty and sound judgement are rare bedfellows, it is important to judge when it is best to obey a rule and when it is preferable to bend or break it.

An investment portfolio is like a garden

Good investors, like good gardeners, thirst for knowledge, gather expertise, revel in diversity and learn from experience. Investment portfolios, like gardens, need constant maintenance. There are routine jobs to be done and emergency tasks that will not wait. An attentive caretaker will cherish, nourish and protect in the full knowledge that if he or she fails to do what is necessary there will be a price to pay.

Like gardens, investments are dependent on an environment that changes: where gardeners look to the seasons, investors look to the economic and market cycles. Like garden plants, investments have periods when they catch the attention – when they are flourishing – but they also need time to be left undisturbed, for preparation, rest and regeneration. Some investments last a long time; others have a shorter life expectancy.

Left to their own devices entirely, investments go

to seed alarmingly quickly. With time and effort, skill and some luck, there are rich rewards to be harvested.